Golden Dreams

Companion to
Hellfires of Grief:
Love Poems

Carlos Eldon Taylor
and
Carol Susan DeVaney-Wong

Golden Dreams

Companion to Hellfires of Grief: Love Poems

©2013 C. Eldon Taylor

ISBN: 0615909809
ISBN-13: 978-0615909806

LCCN: 2013920046

Printed in USA
by CreateSpace
an Amazon.com Company

Published by
C. Eldon Taylor
Henrico, Virginia 23228

to
Taryne Jade

Introduction

Golden Dreams: Companion to Hellfires of Grief: Love Poems is a collection of 111 poems describing the golden dreams shared by Carol Susan and Carlos Eldon after the disembodiment of Carol Susan. Carol Susan reaches from beyond to share her golden healing energy. Carlos Eldon travels to the spirit realm to visit with his beloved in shared golden dreams. *Golden Dreams* is the counterpoint to *Hellfires of Grief: Love Poems* providing Carlos Eldon with the wonderful golden love of his celestial soulmatespiritmate.

The poems are condensed from dream journals starting with the first golden dream of January 5, 2012 and continuing until the 111th golden dream of October 9, 2013. Not all the dreams are golden as some do not include Carol Susan's beautiful radiant golden celestial aura. The overall energy of *Golden Dreams* is golden providing a healing counterpoint to the intense darkness of *Hellfires of Grief*. The poems in *Hellfires of Grief: Love Poems* are lit by the black fires of the hell of loss and grief while

Golden Dreams is illuminated by the celestial golden light of love. Shared golden dreams start the process of healing and provide a glimpse into the realm of spirit. Shared golden dreams spill into the waking time slowly transforming the grief dragon described in *Hellfires of Grief: Love Poems* which covers the first eighteen months of loss and grief. *Hellfires of Grief II: More Love Poems* is currently underway and summarizes the second eighteen months of loss, grief, and healing.

Having a golden rainbow dragon mother goddess and angel as coauthor and muse is a wonderful experience paradoxically the disembodiment of Carol Susan is the worst experience. We have been blessed with shared golden dreams. Carol Susan and Carlos Eldon are pleased to share our healing golden dreams. It is our hope, wish, and intent that sharing our golden dreams will bring a measure of comfort and healing energy to all who read them.

May you be blessed with golden dreams,

Carlos Eldon and Carol Susan

October 31, 2013

Golden Dreams
Table of Contents

First Golden Dream

needed to pick up medicine
at two pharmacies
Carol Susan suddenly appeared
radiant beautiful smiling
looking like a goddess
an angel
celestial version of my beloved
she did not need to speak
I knew she was going to help me
pick up medicine at one pharmacy
so I could go to the other
as words were not needed I thought
"but you're naked don't you think
you should put on some clothes"
Carol Susan laughed her delightful laugh
suddenly had on small black panties
when I realized this was all
she intended to wear
she laughed even more
as she floated off towards the door
I realized without words
she told me I was the only one
who could see her
as she floated down the street
she looked back at me
smiled her wonderful smile
looked beyond happy
a radiant vibrant goddess
I could see her golden energy field
surrounding her
fully illuminated

only wore the black panties
a short while
just to see my reaction
her trickster mode
fully enjoying herself yet
full of compassion and love for me
bathing me in her loving spirit as always
occurred to me the visit would be brief
such different forms
Carol Susan a spirit realm angel goddess
me an old grieving mortal
in the dream I was so happy to see her
so sad after she was gone

after the dream I was so very happy
to experience Carol Susan
in the subtle spirit realm
knowing she had recovered
from her transition
her disembodiment
beyond pain and suffering
experience her as a healing angel
goddess of compassionate love
reaching out to help her loved ones

I cried writing down the dream
thankful my beloved appeared
her gift to me
appearance of her celestial spirit
assuring me of her help
I had been hoping for a dream
expecting a dream
wondering how long it would be
sixty-six days

I call them golden dreams because
Carol Susan's spirit energy field is golden
as my vision has improved
with later dreams
I now see more subtle energy fields
rainbow energy fields
surrounding Carol Susan's spirit body
I still call them golden dreams
blessed with golden dreams
shared with my beloved

first golden dream
January 5, 2012
transcribed July 5, 2013

Young CS Talking

Carol Susan talking to a young girl
Carol Susan is also a young girl
wise beyond her years
Carol Susan overflows with
kindness love understanding
compassion maternal affection
reassuring the other of her value
knew the other needed reassurance
acceptance support love
Carol Susan knows human needs
has perspective sense of humor
an old soul in a young body
already awake to her inner wisdom
at a very young age
love of the Mother
mixed with the wisdom of the
Wise Old Woman
in the dream Carol Susan
was not yet a Maiden
still a young girl
already manifested the attributes
of all three aspects of the feminine
Carol Susan is young and already wise
young and already maternal
a young girl but already a maiden
beautiful loving wise
wonderful to hear her voice
feel her energy
feel her love
experience her soul

Second Golden Dream
January 6, 2012
transcribed July 14, 2013

Golden Boo Boo

I am in the center of a very old
yellow stone plaza
near the fountain in the center
Carol Susan appears
at one of the entrances
young beautiful radiant smiling
small girl with her
wanted to see me
Carol Susan is wearing
the blue and red dress I made her
when she was pregnant
she said
"I've got a boo boo on my breast"
my first thought was to say
that's no boo boo it's your nipple
but since the first dream
I say what I feel in my heart
not my head's response
I say
"Well I'll have to kiss it and
make it all better"
Carol Susan smiles
we approach
I kiss her boo boo
golden energy aura of a goddess
Carol Susan knew she did not
have a boo boo
wanted to comfort me
pleased I disregarded my head response
responded from my heart
Carol Susan shared her spirit energy

her celestial love
embraced me with her celestial energy
healing embrace
healing love
healing dream
blessed by golden dreams

Third Golden Dream
January 15, 2012
transcribed July 14, 2013

Golden Cocoon Ride

I am riding with Carol Susan
some kind of vehicle
going very fast
on a roadway
vehicle makes no noise
not a car
no wheels no steering wheel
no instruments
Carol Susan controls the vehicle
by her intent
she exclaims
"oh look lets go over there
and we can meet   "
(name I do not remember)
suddenly the vehicle whips
off the roadway
through a grassy area
woodland path
off the beaten path
Carol Susan is happy to be
on the natural path
by now I realize the vehicle
is Carol Susan's energy field
she is giving me a tour
taking me to meet some one
sitting together as companions
I am a visitor Carol Susan is home
vehicle her golden energy cocoon
after my initial surprise
I relaxed enjoying being with
Carol Susan in her golden cocoon

which is her home
felt like my home too
wonderful experience
being with Carol Susan
in her energy field
after I relaxed is when
Carol Susan whipped off
the beaten path
she was very happy I was
adding energy to the golden cocoon
Carol Susan was beautiful radiant
a goddess
not as bright as in the first golden dream
or perhaps my subtle eyes
were working better
a wonderful visit
riding with Carol Susan
in her golden energy cocoon
blessed with golden dreams

Fourth Golden Dream
January 17, 2012
transcribed July 15, 2013

Dark Shadows

Carol Susan and I are at our favorite inn
celebrating our anniversary
Carol Susan is in her mortal form
she looks beautiful in her mortal form way
does not appear ill
yet a shadow over the dream
over the celebration
we both know it is our last time
we will be at the inn together
with Carol Susan in her physical body
Carol Susan is making the best of it
I sense darkness
something ominous
Carol Susan already knows
does not speak about it
enjoying the moment
hard for me to ignore
underlying dark shadows
I think the inn has lost some of its charm
food comes
food is cold
we alert the wait person
promises to correct the situation
immediately
Carol Susan and I sit and talk
so many wonderful memories
quiet times
sharing times
at our favorite inn

dream moves to the next morning

at breakfast
one of the inn's owners
comes to apologize for the cold food
we both tell her it is no problem
she insists Carol Susan go to the gift shop
pick out something to make amends
for the cold food
Carol Susan goes off
visiting with the owner
I think Carol Susan will bring
something for me
she returns with a handmade cigar box
holding a few maduro cigars
I thank Carol Susan for the gift
we talk comfortably over breakfast
in the light of day
the darkness of the night before
does not seem as bad
wonderful to see Carol Susan
happy to be visiting with people
bring me a gift
enjoying life
even though she already knew
something is not right with her body
not yet manifested
for others to see
Carol Susan already knew
while not nearly as sensitive
I was aware of some vague
shadow of darkness

towards the end of the dream
thinking about the symbolism of the box
holding the cigars I said to myself

"you know sometimes a cigar is just a cigar
and sometimes a box is just a box
and sometimes they are not"
Carol Susan was fully aware of the symbolism
enjoyed my obvious pondering of the gift
holding the box with reverence
a sacred object
I remarked "what a wonderful treasure"
Carol Susan laughed
she understood my reference to the
sacredness of the vessel
wonderful moment shared
with my soulmate
now spiritmate

while the dream had a dark shadow
Carol Susan's attitude was positive
focused on living a high definition life
enjoying life's simple pleasures
living in the moment
teaching by example
teaching even in my dreams

Carol Susan's golden energy
always present
even during the dark times
now in golden dreams
shared with my beloved
blessed with golden dreams

Fifth Golden Dream
January 23, 2012
transcribed July 15, 2013

Jealousy

floating near a school
see Carol Susan age 17
walking in the hall with
a young man about her age
his arm draped over her shoulder
she is smiling walking together
her smile does not appear full force
but she seems happy enough

I always claimed not to be jealous
yet I knew I did not like the thought
of Carol Susan with anyone else
always affected an enlightened
non-possessive attitude
Carol Susan knew I did not believe
I was not possessive
greedy jealous
now in the hellfires of grief
my frailties
my dark side
dark dream shows up
not a golden dream

I always told myself
Carol Susan was happiest with me
more radiant
more golden energy
her smile lighting up all the space
around her including me

I am grateful beyond measure
Carol Susan picked me
as her life companion

yes I was and am jealous
possessive greedy
in my mortal realm body
even after her disembodiment
irrational mortal frailties
golden dreams are not contaminated
golden cocoon is pure love
yet when awake I am greedy for
more golden dreams
more golden memories
but have to settle for more burning
in the hellfires of grief
the impurities fueled by
my jealousy possessiveness
and greed
my longing for more golden dreams

Black Dream Six
January 30, 2012
transcribed July 25, 2013

Grandmother's Stone

vague dream about a stone
a special stone I needed to locate
remembered your Abuelita Maria's stone
she used it for many years
you always kept her stone near
talked about it from time to time
you and Abuelita Maria were very close
I found the special stone
put Abuelita Maria's stone at the shrine
Grandmother energy at the shrine
special stone honored at the shrine
ancestors honored
glad to locate the special stone
place it at the shrine
know you and Maria are pleased

Dream Seven
January 31, 2012
transcribed July 25, 2013

Golden Spirit Merger

contaminated by my physical eyes physical mind
first think Carol Susan in a hotel room
as my spirit eyes fully open
knew I was seeing from
Carol Susan's spirit eyes
two spirit bodies merged
room was Carol Susan's
spirit realm sanctuary
visited many times in other dreams
merged I could feel Carol Susan's
love and compassion for me
compassion for my grief
longing
missing her physical being
her memories of our times together
vivid intense yet peaceful
acceptance appreciation
love joy
no grief like I am experiencing
yet Carol Susan remembers
her physical body
small remnant of sadness
at the loss of her physical body
small because her compassion
is so large including for herself

so the question I had asked
the day before as well as
many days before
if she was angry
for my short comings

failings limitations
not following path with heart
staying in my head too much
getting caught up in mundane matters

Carol Susan's answer
to welcome me to merge
with her spirit body
experience her spirit soul
merge spirit bodies
when my spirit eyes opened
looking out with our combined spirit eyes
beyond an answer
as our combined spirit eyes looked inward
Carol Susan's love and compassion
overwhelmed me with gratitude

words can never describe
the wonder
the bliss of seeing from
Carol Susan's spirit eyes
merging spirit bodies
two become one
in the golden cocoon
grateful beyond words for this
transcendent golden dream

Eighth Golden Dream
February 6, 2012
transcribed July 25, 2013

Celestial Wedding

Carol Susan and I are traveling to Panama
our anniversary coincides with our trip
I ask Carol Susan if she will marry me again
in a Catholic Church in Panama
Carol Susan smiles accepts my proposal
comments church will not sanction
such an event
I suggest we celebrate our recommittment
without blessing of church authorities
Mother will bless renewal of our vows
Carol Susan smiles in agreement

Carol Susan in her wedding dress
I in a formal tuxedo
Carol Susan is lovely beautiful
beyond words
golden radiant

scene shifts
we are spirit bodies
dressed in celestial wedding clothes
Carol Susan a goddess
we are relaxing in a spirit realm
woodland meadow
appears if only the two of us are present
then a large number of spirits gather
to witness the event
space around us filled with presence
of so many spirits
joyful to be attending the event
Carol Susan and I are joyful

smiling and laughing

the event shifts to beach
Carol Susan and I are holding one another
in our spirit forms
without words
declare again we are spiritmates
always forever and beyond
space around us filled with
layer upon layer of spirits
all of our ancestors
from the beginning
stretching into the future
and beyond
witness the golden celestial wedding

wonderful golden dream
wonderful golden memories
nourished by golden energy
of spirit realm
my soulmate
spiritmate
and our ancestors
blessed with golden dreams

Golden Dream Nine
February 13, 2012
transcribed July 29, 2013

Fixing Little Dragon

riding in little dragon
Carol Susan's dark green Audi Fox
little dragon stopped running
coasted to a stop on side of road
Carol Susan steered
I pushed little dragon
further off the highway
atmosphere very relaxed
emergency repairs
I diagnosed problem
made repairs
happened a few times with little dragon
traveling in physical realm
each time Carol Susan steered
while I pushed then
fixed little dragon
very comfortable confident partnership
fixing little dragon

Dream Ten
March 12, 2012
transcribed August 12, 2013

Door Bell

7:00 AM
woke hearing Carol Susan say
"Eldon, that's the door bell"
Carol Susan did not say
door bell was ringing
not cottage door bell
realize I do not know
where door bell is
where door is
where door opens to
who is behind door
reminds me of trip
in golden cocoon
Carol Susan taking to meet someone
suspect the door is my heart
grief opens door
to subtle spirit realm
and
my beloved

Dream Eleven
March 24, 2012
transcribed August 12, 2013

Sacred Place

discover a small cavern passage
leading to ancient alter
neutral atmosphere
alter empty
ancient sacred site
beyond alter small passageway
leading to larger natural space
walled with stone blocks
attempt to hide natural sacred place
ancient sacred space
decide to get rubber mallet
convinced stone wall has secret door
opening to ancient sacred place where
Mother Goddess was celebrated

broken hearted from
disembodiment of my soulmate
searching to access
sacred spirit realm
hidden behind man made wall
know Mother Goddess the way
to access spirit realm
subtle body travel
to sacred spirit realm
and my beloved

Dream Twelve
April 20, 2012
transcribed August 12, 2013

Goddess in a Thermal Dress

setting in country store with a few people
Carol Susan enters in a thermal dress
I tell the others "it's my sweetheart"
go to her we kiss embrace
Carol Susan is smiling radiant beautiful
goddess in a thermal dress
light purple with purple flowers
Carol Susan shows me matching
thermal turtleneck shirt
says "if I get this you might have to
give up being outside on Mondays"
shows me label "Rainy Mondays"
we both laugh I say
"I would be very happy to stay inside with you
thermal material never looked so good"
goddess in a thermal dress

dream reminds me of best moments
in physical realm
time slowed disappeared
only the moment existed
merged together in our golden cocoon
blessed with golden dreams
new experiences new memories
with my beloved

Golden Dream Thirteen
May 4, 2012
transcribed August 12, 2013

Grieving Together

Carol Susan has cancer
then she was small a child
very sad crying
I was holding her
comforting her as best I could
we were both crying
then we were both small
both nurturing each other
mothering each other
comforting each other
as best as we could
both crying
holding each other
loving each other
always forever and beyond

Dream Fourteen
June 13, 2012
transcribed August 12, 2013

Celestial Grief

woke up at 5 am
with tears in my eyes
streaming down my face
very vivid intense dream
Carol Susan and Carlos Eldon
grieving together in spirit realm
golden spirit beings
higher spirit selves
grieving Carol Susan's illness
Carol Susan's disembodiment
her pain and suffering
her distress at leaving
her loved ones behind
two celestial beings
crying holding comforting
loving one another
no words needed
spirit realm more complex
complicated than I ever imagined
relationship of soul and spirit
much more complex
mysterious paradoxical
cannot be explained with words
spirit may transcend and soar
soul swims in the depths of the
primordial sea
with loving nurturance
of the Great Mother
soul and spirit coexist
as above so below
as within so without

words cannot describe
my experience of
Carol Susan and Carlos Eldon
golden celestial beings
celestial grieving
celestial grief
compassion for those left behind
in the physical realm
spirit realm much more complex
than I could ever imagine
angels grieve
gods and goddesses grieve
celestial beings grieve
comforting to share
celestial grieving

Golden Dream Fifteen
June 15, 2012
transcribed August 12, 2013

Shocking Wedding

Carol Susan and I are getting married
large event in a cathedral
like National Shrine to Mary,
Mother of Human Kind
Carol Susan's favorite in US
Carol Susan beyond beautiful
radiant golden goddess
as service about to start
four chaps enter with intent
to disrupt ceremony
I smile at Carol Susan saying
"this will only take a moment"
produce powerful stun gun
then chaps are on the floor
I held out my hand to Carol Susan
we proceed down the aisle
Carol Susan clearly delighted
I was prepared decisive
we walked down the aisle
hand in hand into our future
our past shocked into submission
well behind us

Golden Dream Sixteen
June 16, 2012
transcribed August 12, 2013

New Shoes

in the dream I am preparing
to give a talk to a group
ask Carol Susan to please
pick out some new shoes
for me
she agrees but advises me
new shoes may be uncomfortable
I agree but mention that my shoes
are worn looking
and
I want to make a good impression

Carol Susan returns as I am dressing
gives me a pair of elegant new shoes
put them on they are perfect
Carol Susan smiles

Golden Dream Seventeen
July 18, 2012
transcribed August 12, 2013

•

Black Gold Cocoon

Carol Susan and I are on the back
of a very large creature like substance
black as night
soft warm not fur
magic like substance
we are on the ocean
huge black creature like substance
moving with no movement
movement by intent
black creature like substance
very friendly towards
Carol Susan and me
we are riding on a huge
black cocoon
as I term the mysterious substance
ocean very calm
cooperating with black cocoon
we approach an island
black cocoon glides up on the beach
we do not disembark
we are very comfortable
part of the black cocoon
black cocoon part of us
if golden cocoon is spirit
black cocoon is soul
our merged combined souls
combined with the soul
of Mother Earth
Mother Earth's soul
providing black gold energy
black golden ride

setting together on black gold cocoon
no sadness
no grieving
peaceful relaxed companionship
respite from hellfires of grief
suggests dark path
provides intense healing energy

very grateful for this magical
black golden dream shared
with my beloved
and
magical black golden cocoon

Black Golden Dream Eighteen
July 23, 2012
transcribed August 12, 2013

Empty House

I am outside a frame house
Carol Susan's voice says
"she is missing...not here"
then screams
"there is a pair of pants
on the floor in the bathroom"
I enter the house
fearing scene of violence
realize violence already occurred
I say "she is gone"
start to cry
Carol Susan's disembodied voice
cries with me
house empty
except for her disembodied voice
her artifacts
our loving energies
sharing our grief together
at the scene of the crime

Dream Nineteen
August 6, 2012
transcribed August 14, 2013

Serpent Dragon Panther

many men carrying huge serpent
from jungle to a resting place
serpent white with light tan
men treated serpent as
sacred being
naga
placed head in cradle
rubbing head
serpent asleep
men trying to feed serpent dark
liquid
serpent's eyes opened

now serpent looks like
monster skull in the cradle
if looked at properly
can see eyes other features
looks like giant dragon
midnight blue dragon
men rocking dragon's head
pouring dark liquid in its mouth
dragon started to purr
dragon opened its eyes
looked at me
friendly but detached
men using small shovels
removing debris from dragon's mouth
placed stones from mouth into cradle
dragon continued to purr
men surprised
did not know dragons purred

I was not surprised
know dragon was happy to see me
I was very happy to see dragon

only a portion of dragon
existed in dreamtime
most of dragon
existed in otherwhere
at first I could only see
dragon's skull
then dragon's head
when dragon's eyes opened
I could see dragon
into otherwhere
dragon's body celestial dark blue
with golden energy
dragon's purr wonderful sound

dream shifted
visiting friends in the country
they ask if I would like to exercise
their cat
said exercise is a strange word
to use for playing with a cat
they told me I had not seen
their cat
cat appeared
huge black panther
we looked at each other
I smiled
knew the cat
cat jumped on me
we rolled around
cat licked me

we were reunited
friends
cat at least my size
magical creature
change colors size
other attributes aspects
not a dreamtime creature
celestial creature

three magical creatures
much more than they appeared
teachers advisors allies
magical friends from otherwhere

Golden Dream Twenty
August 11, 2012
transcribed August 14, 2013

One Word

dream of one word
Carol Susan said
"Eldon"
her voice
mind to mind
telling me she loves me
one word all she needed
total complete unconditional love
one word
pure love

blessed with golden dreams
shared with my beloved

Golden Dream Twenty-one
August 13, 2012
transcribed August 14, 2013

Curious Visitor

cleaning up patch of weeds
corner of backyard
looked across field
saw large ant like beast
on top a green container
creature crimson three feet long
aware I was looking
attracted by my energy
launched into the air
thought creature
would fly into me
perhaps get hurt
tossed some dirt into the air
diverted flight path
flew on by
I was pleased neither
of us got hurt
spectators impressed

telling dream healer suggested
beast may have been bring gifts
said I did not like the delivery system
decided next time I will say hello
mind to mind
no blame

Dream Twenty-two
August 21, 2012
transcribed August 14, 2013

Lower Level Tour

my guide takes me to lower level
of spirit realm
overlooking another guide
seeks out a being they wrestle
no one is hurt both energy beings
evenly matched
eventually being is exhausted
changes shape small energy being
sharp teeth furry body
wrestling energy workout
guide assisting being to
discover aspects of itself
assisting others to
learn about themselves
act of compassion loving kindness
my guide did not say much
at first I was concerned by combat
wanted to get involved
my guide said
"I brought you here to watch -watch"
my guide seemed pleased
by my response to the scene
my compassion
for all participants
all beings

Dream Twenty-three
September 5, 2012
transcribed August 14, 2013

Sea Rescue

Carol Susan in her early 20's
beautiful radiant goddess
floating in ocean
demonic energy behind her
sky lit with red orange glow
I am on small boat
throw her a rope
think "grab hold"
she does I pull her into the boat
we embrace
demonic energy dissipated
when Carol Susan grabbed rope
disappeared when we embraced
constituted our golden cocoon
protection for us both

rope our lifeline to each other
once our lifelines touched
again
fates smiled said
"it is good"
dream compensates for my
questioning my value
conformation we are one another's
life lines
continues in subtle form

Golden Dream Twenty-four
September 17, 2012
transcribed August 14, 2013

Spirit Stones

in room with stones
younger person with me
recognize as my higher self
realize he is my teacher
higher self telling me
about charging stones
in sunlight
in moonlight
stones shaped like rods
large diamond rod
large ruby rod
suspect my higher self
call him Carlos Eldon
manifested the stones
spirit stones
energy stones
healing stones
master teacher
teaching his smaller self
about energy

blessed with master teachers
blessed with golden dreams

Golden Dream Twenty-five
October 1, 2012
transcribed August 15, 2013

45

Crystal Orb

ball in my computer mouse
transforms into clear quartz orb
frees itself from mouse
travels around my office
have to round up orb
scold it for being naughty
wondering off
orb has a mind of its own
yet is also part of me
always on my person
or near by
replaces regular mouse ball
then wonders off
so I will attend to it
locate it not work on other things
orb only found when it wants to be
seems to enjoy the game of hide and seek
unfair advantage becoming invisible
does not often appear in physical realm

dream shifts to wooded park
rascal orb wondered off
small clearing of grass leaves
worried I may have trouble
finding orb in larger space
part of me knows it is a game
we play together
so worry less
play along
think I could do better
if I had a rake

suddenly holding large leaf rake
then think orb could
pass through the rake
if it wanted to
think all I really need to do
intend to see orb
recover the rascal
become more relaxed in the dream
figured lesson orb teaching
not hide and seek
how to use intent

Dream Twenty-six
October 7, 2012
transcribed August 18, 2013

Sanctuary

visit Carol Susan's private sanctuary
spirit realm sanctuary
been there many times before
large room glass wall over looking garden
room mostly white abstract
zen like space
table and two chairs
crystal vase one flower
expansive room no clutter
always been welcomed
when I arrive Carol Susan
not there
busy otherwhere
stayed awhile
enjoying sanctuary
disappointed Carol Susan
otherwhere
another time

Dream Twenty-seven
October 21, 2012
transcribed August 19, 2012

Too Much Life

in mountains with native people
perhaps South America
they gather eating and drinking
told my guide people looked like
they had too much of something
guide chuckled
then thought they have
too much of life
too much direct experience
compared to my indirect
vicarious experience
my guide chuckled again
seems easy to over emphasize
knowledge of the mind
ignore knowledge of the heart and soul
direct experience

Dream Twenty-eight
November 7, 2012
transcribed August 18, 2013

Spirit Couple

vague outline of tall woman
walked past me into another room
followed her
asked where she came from
how she got in
she answered
"oh I've been here for a while
my husband, you know, is psychic
and he said everything is fixed"
saw hands lying on the table
vague outline of tall man dark hair
woman had auburn hair
worn like Carol Susan
long luxurious hair
long elegant fingers
man's hands on black journal
on the black table
very comfortable with spirit couple
very familiar even if vague
afterwards I wondered
why I did not ask
better questions
what was fixed
thank them
glad spirit couple came to visit
glad I remembered the dream
blessed with golden dreams

Golden Dream Twenty-nine
December 4, 2012
transcribed August 18, 2013

Rescue

Carol Susan and I are in a canoe
traveling on tropical jungle river
lush jungle foliage
crystal clear river
no signs of civilization
come upon a young boy
sitting on bank
appears lost
separated from his tribe
offer to bring him along
he accepts
we are traveling along
on river
as dream fades
good feeling to rescue
young boy

Golden Dream Thirty
December 9, 2012
transcribed August 18, 2013

Path With Heart

sitting at kitchen table
talking to young girl
giving her advice
about her problems
advice from the head
rational logical
problem solving approach
not understanding her need
to vent
be heard
needing an emotional response
response from the heart
not head logical rational response
frustrated with my responses
not feeling understood
left to find her mother
approach of sky gods
not the path with heart
too often my path
becoming clear
path with heart
dark earth path
night path
moonlit path
way of the Mother
path with heart
confirmed in my dreams

Dream Thirty-one
December 11, 2012
transcribed August 19, 2013

Leaving

Carol Susan tells me she is leaving
I am in shock disbelief
tells me she is sick
I start crying
ask if she can stay
if there is anything I can do
she tells me "no
there is nothing to be done"
I cry and cry
promise to always love her
promise to do anything for her
Carol Susan says
"your love is enough"

nightmare dream
awaken to nightmare reality
Carol Susan's disembodiment
only golden part of dream
Carol Susan saying
"your love is enough"
my love is
always forever and beyond

Dream Thirty-two
December 13, 2012
transcribed August 19, 2013

Ally

woman knew long ago appeared
asked how I was doing
if I needed any assistance
told her as well as could be expected
considering the circumstances
told me she had some money
she would share with me
thanked her for her offer
did not need money
her kindness was enough
one of my allies
one of my ancestors
perhaps from another
life time

later thinking about the dream
decided currency offered
not physical realm money
spirit realm currency
energy
love
I was too literal
next offer
I will accept
accepted kindness
so no blame

Dream Thirty-three
December 14, 2012
transcribed August 22, 2013

Guide

guide to young bride
visiting family of groom
women are teasing her
light hearted teasing
bride concerned
advise her to look
beneath the surface
women of the clan
inviting her into their fold
she understands
comfort level improves
warms to clan women
my guidance helpful
good fortune

Dream Thirty-four
December 20, 2012
transcribed August 22, 2013

No More Tests

Carol Susan in small room
hospital setting
I am in waiting room
just down the hall
I became distressed
knew things not going right
went to her room
she was not there
staff told me she had decided
to run few errands
looked to see
none of her things
were there
knew she was not coming back
very distressed
frantic
need to leave to find her
leaving as dream faded

Dream Thirty-five
January 4, 2013
transcribed August 22, 2013

Subtle Realm Visit

Carol Susan and I exploring country side
came upon embassy in remote area
impressive structure surrounded
with iron fence
not interested in building
went left discovered
passage into grounds gardens
found construction site
superficial on surface
if look with subtle vision
huge underground structure
man with white hair beard appeared
ask what we were doing
told him looking at underground structure
he was pleased we could see
into subtle realm
guide invited us on a tour
told us about sacred site
subtle realm not really beneath physical realm
superimposed comingled concurrent
if you look with subtle vision
threshold place with my beloved
sharing subtle spirit realm
exploring sacred place
blessed by its guardian

Golden Dream Thirty-six
January 6, 2013
transcribed August 22, 2013

Golden Guardians

sitting in elegant classic car
silver with black top black leather interior
sitting beside me beautiful young woman
skin the color of radiant gold cinnamon
we were talking observing
around us people were looking for
someone named Eldon Taylor
I said "I am glad that I am not that chap
he seems to be attracting a lot of attention"
occurred to me I might be or have been
that chap or would be one day
I looked at myself
young man
same radiant gold cinnamon skin
as young woman
as if looking into another dimension
I could see both from his eyes
as well as from above the scene
couple seemed like guardians
well above the energy level
of the rest of the scene
neither couple nor car
were what they seemed
suspected couple and car
only visible to me

Golden Dream Thirty-seven
January 8, 2013
transcribed August 22, 2013

Little Blue White Fish

first thought little blue white fish
swimming in water
sleek radiant white creature
like a giant porpoise
swimming in air
swam into belly of large rubber whale
when little blue white fish
entered the rubber whale
toy whale bulged wiggled rippled
then little blue white fish
would pop out
delighted by the trick
I watched for a long time
little blue white fish
did not seem to tire of the game
occurred to me
little blue white fish
could assume any shape
it wished
enjoyed being born
from rubber toy whale
over and over
chrysalis to butterfly
metamorphosis
shedding its skin
becoming a new creature
showing me the game
over and over
important message
rebirth motif
at one point I wondered how

little blue white fish
managed to pop out
with such ease
little blue white fish
demonstrated in slow motion
transformed the membrane
of rubber toy whale
crossed the membrane
like crossing the veil
little blue white fish
as my guide
another manifestation of
rainbow dragon fish
manifestation of my soul
playing in the cosmic sea

Golden Dream Thirty-eight
January 9, 2013
transcribed August 22, 2013

Obscure Benefits

Carol Susan and I sitting in our kitchen
at our old round cherry table
Carol Susan telling me about two
obscure benefits
for certain illnesses
both benefits have names
do not remember them
types of disability benefits
do not remember details
Carol Susan is very happy to be
telling me what she learned
I am very happy to be
visiting with her
she is a mother goddess
goddess of middle years
beautiful radiant
golden energy of her love
fills the room and beyond

happy to remember another
golden dream
visiting my beloved in golden dreams
blessed with golden dreams

Golden Dream Thirty-nine
January 14, 2013
transcribed August 25, 2013

Rubber Floor

at work I spray the floor
with black rubber coating
creates a jell like fatigue mat
my employers are upset
suspend me while they
investigate my conduct
one of my staff promoted
tells me my employers
unhappy with my pace
too many changes too fast
time for me to move on
I wonder to myself
if I can roll up
rubber jell mat
take it along with me
rubber floor has healing properties
insulates from toxicity
offers some protection
enjoy the image
rolling up the rubber floor
taking it with me
sometimes need protection
from more than the elements

Dream Forty
January 19, 2013
transcribed August 25, 2013

Grandmother

talking to an older woman
seems very familiar
known her for many many life times
she smiles warmly as I think this
telling her about the kittens
she tells me all our helpers
assisted in selecting the kittens
healers companions
help with the dark times
they are all pleased with results

occurs to me old woman
one of my spirit guides
she smiles warmly agrees
holds out her arms
we embrace
she an energy being who wears
old woman's body
like a garment
merger of energy bodies wonderful
way beyond wonderful
think way better than sex
she chuckles tells me
good to see I was regaining
some of my irreverent sense of humor
since I was connected to my physical body
comparison could be expected
told her that I had not read of guides
merging with their charges all that often
she smiled warmly told me
I was both spoiled and in need of comfort

as loss of my soulmate's physical body
huge blow to me
even more so that they had expected
thanked her for being with me
for her assistance
she pleased by my expression of gratitude
she then answered my unspoken question
told me she worked mostly in the
background since I had my soulmate with me
in her physical body
so focused on her
often did not pay much attention
to anything else
of course I agreed
regretfully admitted did not always
pay attention to excellent advice
of my soulmate either
my guide smiled told me
yes I had always been rather head strong
but was doing OK
she tells me they are aware of my
regrets and remorse
pleased my heart is open
I am deeply loved
forgiveness is not necessary
except self-forgiveness
she told me if it helps for me
to hear her say it
they all forgive me
she chuckles warmly as she says this
provides me with the image of our
energy embrace
energy merger
reminds me of another dream

where I am looking from Carol Susan's
spirit eyes
unconditional love overwhelming
even with her physical realm memories
that I was sometimes
less that she might have preferred
unconditional love cleared away tarnish
darkness
wonderful experience
wonderful memory
my guide smiles warmly at my memory agrees
self forgiveness while still in my physical body
more difficult challenge

very happy to have this dream visit with
my guide
she has been my guide a very long time
great affection for me as one of her
children
I have great affection for her as my
grandmother
a very high level energy being
not going to attempt to claim
Kuan Yin as my guide
but if not Her one of Her
favorite daughters
often told Carol Susan for many years
she was a favorite daughter
of the trio of Goddesses of Compassion
Kuan Yin White Tara Mother Mary
my grandmother guide
did not dispute my musing
She and the Others
enjoyed my discomfort

when I thought about comparing
embracing the Goddess with sex
They knew I was not really
all that uncomfortable

blessed to remember this dream visit
with my grandmother
blessed to have such a wonderful master
as my guide
blessed with golden dreams
possession in great measure

Golden Dream Forty-one
January 21, 2013
transcribed August 25, 2013

Grandfather

sitting with very old man
reminds me of my grandfather
who never became really old
I told him stories of my memories
of my grandfather
old man seemed happy to visit
hear memory stories
possessions had no interest
to old man
loving memories made him smile
nod his head
too old to be my grandfather
in his physical embodiment
perhaps another guide
me as an old man
we sit comfortably visiting
me and old man

Dream Forty-two
January 22, 2013
transcribed August 25, 2013

Transformed Space

discover unused suite of rooms
seem like work area study area
one room has large table
like a meeting room
rooms drab unused
empty no energy
I look about then leave

decide I want to return
soon as I think about returning
back in space again
space different
evidence of people
one room converted to supply room
food and beverages
more light brighter colors
hear young voices laughing talking
from meeting room
taking a break
tell them to enjoy themselves
as I leave
they wave thank me
for refreshments
could feel improved energy
youthful atmosphere
enthusiasm of youth
nice transformation

Dream Forty-three
January 26, 2013
transcribed August 25, 2013

Healing Crystals

showing Carol Susan how I use
two large crystals
diamond and amethyst
to assist recently disembodied souls
clean away any darkness
tarnish debris
crystals concentrate healing light
illuminate darkness
provide healing energy
told Carol Susan I did not
really need crystals
used them as props
souls who had yet to learn
how to self illuminate
more comfortable with
me using crystals

upon waking I thought
that is what I wanted to be
able to do in physical realm
but could not remember how

Carol Susan pleased to watch
my demonstration
she did not need my healing
in spirit realm

Golden Dream Forty-four
January 27, 2013
transcribed August 25, 2013

CS's Self Healing

Carol Susan's recently disembodied soul
while radiant beautiful
contained some darkness from
her physical incarnation
physical embodiment
when she returned to spirit realm
merged with her higher self
her energy illuminated
her returning soul
she spontaneously healed herself
her healer her higher self
I witnessed her self healing
then we shared family hug
all illuminating all
golden rainbow dragons
sharing energy of our love

blessed to remember this golden dream
blessed with golden dreams
shared with my beloved

Golden Dream Forty-five
January 27, 2013
transcribed August 25, 2013

Maya's Head

looking at kitten Maya
notice line around her head
at the bottom of her neck
Maya heard my thoughts
said "yes my head is a cover detachable"
she demonstrated
put her paws to each side of her head
lifted off her kitten head like a mask
underneath a light being energy being
head of light very old face
very wise being
she said "see it is easy to do"
held out kitten mask
then put in on again
I was not shocked by this display
knew Maya to be more than she appeared
her guardian old wise
fairy cat energy being
Merlin did not demonstrate
reveal the light being beneath
know he has one
his is younger the student
Maya's an old master the teacher
both are healers

grateful for this wonderful dream
perhaps my improved spirit vision
not a dream a vision waking dream

Golden Dream Forty-six
January 29, 2013
transcribed August 25, 2013

Many Mergers

dream many memories
Carol Susan and I merge
in physical realm
energy bodies
physical bodies
intense shared energy
transforms Carol Susan
from one embodied face body
to another
many life times of merging
many life times of loving
then merging of embodied self
with higher self
merger of goddess god
heaven on earth
return to paradise
light beings merge
energy beings merge
golden rainbow dragons merge
yin yang merge
beyond words
beyond physical realm

Golden Dream Forty-seven
February 10, 2013
transcribed August 25, 2013

Energy Triangle

young woman demonstrating
healing energy triangle
tips of two thumbs together
tips of two forefingers touch
creates a triangle three energies
right side right forefinger
left side left forefinger
combined middle of thumbs
creates third energy
three energies blend
form energy ray energy beam
concentrated healing energy
pure illumination

intense healing energy
instantly detox all toxicity
heal all levels of energy bodies physical
body completely
be too much healing
remove incentive for self healing
solution to only heal one energy level
leave rest for self healing
young woman did not really need to
configure physical triangle
pure intent enough
celestial healing power

Dream Forty-eight
February 13, 2013
transcribed August 25, 2013

Another Time

I am a common citizen
in love with noble born woman
my beloved Carol Susan
different name
different face
different body
same energy essence
same soul
another time
nobleman friend charged with
discouraging me from my
interest in noble woman
takes me as friendly captive
I refuse to renounce my love
for noble born woman
become an enemy of the state
held for trial
told rescue mission under way
stay calm
dream ends without
conclusion

Dream Forty-nine
February 18, 2013
transcribed August 25, 2013

Withering Left Arm

discover my left arm withering up
remember Carol Susan telling me
if I did not get enough love
I would wither up like a prune
so my left side is withering up
my receiving side
where you slept for many years
nurturing one another in our sleep
in our dreams

dream telling me I am
not fully open to subtle spirit realm
nurturance
still focused on your physical realm
nurturance
no withering in golden dreams

Dream Fifty
March 2, 2013
transcribed August 25, 2013

Making Preparations

driving around in my car
running errands
determine need to return home
arriving see strange woman
in hall looking for boxes
tells me she is helping
Carol Susan sort out stuff
young girl appears tells me
Carol Susan in a bad mood
I should stay away
I know Carol Susan does not feel well
physically ill
not in a bad mood
I go to her
hold her
she is happy I am there
as she takes on very unhappy task
purging her stuff
making preparations
for leaving
her disembodiment
final leaving of her physical body
on the surface I seem to be OK
holding up just fine
as does Carol Susan
offering my support
my assistance
just being there
inside my heart aches
intense pain
my suffering soul deep

as is hers
for Carol Susan purging
making preparations
acts of love
labor of love
very focused
I knew she was as sad
as I was
doing what she needed to do
leaving things as tidy as possible
taking care of her family
making preparations
for her disembodiment

Dream Fifty-one
March 4, 2013
August 25, 2013

Carol Susan Whispering

old friend retiring
asks me to help
clean out her office
since I do not know what is hers
I ask questions
she starts to tell stories
about memories each object evokes
at some point I tell her a few
of my moving stories
until Carol Susan whispers
my friend does not want to hear my stories
needs support
someone to listen to her stories
just be there as she struggles
with her retirement
next phase of her life
so I listen ask a few questions
provide support
listen
thankful for Carol Susan's whisper
thankful for her presence

Golden Dream Fifty-two
March 8, 2013
transcribed August 28, 2013

Young Woman Old Man

young woman holding celestial court
radiant beautiful goddess
of compassion
judging a group of people
her judgments serve to help people
better look at themselves
determine how they can do better
natural response being in her presence
only need to be in her energy field
to want to improve
perhaps she speaks directly
to each person
mind to mind
likely not necessary
her love compassion
overwhelm resistance
celestial healer

I am watching from a distance
old man purposely invisible
dressed in simple dark robe
not black or purple
black rainbow
underground rainbow
my purpose
provide support
not really needed
appreciated just the same
young woman dressed in white gown
illuminated with her golden energy
goddess energy

she finishes her work
approaches me
says "OK grandfather time to go"
mind to mind
I tell her
time is a meaningless concept
only confuses
adds pain
she smiles
only using as figure of speech
still some souls
need the concept of time
otherwise they would become
lost in river of past present future
where all streams merge cross
backwards forwards
side to side
up down
all directions at once
yet no direction
center the still point
where time does not exist
ocean of timelessness
some call the void
for want of a better word
as good a word as any
for the mysteries
we both smile at our exchange
played with these concepts
many times before
being embodied sucks one into
the vortex of time
whirlpools of time
conversation light playful

underlying the words
celestial level love
celestial level compassion
between young woman old man
golden energy
golden love
golden dream
blessed with golden dreams

Golden Dream Fifty-three
March 10, 2013
transcribed August 28, 2013

Note: Golden Dream Fifty-three inspiration for *Time and the Mystic*,
Hellfires I, page 259

Cosmic Riverboat

take small luxury boat cruise
to tropical island
wander around
looking at nature's wonders
occurs to me boat
will be leaving soon
return to dock
discover boat gone
island set up for day tours
no accommodations
ask about large riverboat
at dock
told for working class
not tourists
had no amenities
approach riverboat
see if they had space available
captain said "yes there is one seat
no one usually wants to take it
we call it the pilot's seat
you can ride there if you are willing"
told her that would be fine
trip from mainland had been smooth
so pilots chair an acceptable option
to return to mainland
captain told me riverboat
took a bit of a different way
to return as some passengers
lived on other islands
needed to be dropped off on the way
told me I better strap down

seemed bit over dramatic
but I followed directions
pilot's chair at bow
provided unobstructed view
pilot's chair had four point restraints
constructed of heavy duty materials
like race cars
thought captain's sense of humor
working folk seem surprised
to see obvious tourist
even more surprised to see
tourist climbing into pilot's chair
surprise converted to concern
when I strapped myself in
worker's seats well back
from sides of riverboat
with standard three point restraints
thought captain must be safety focused
captain ask if I was ready
later realized the question
asked mind to mind
told her I was ready
she chuckled said
"well then hold on for the ride"
thought captain had strange
sense of humor
riverboat left dock
all smooth for awhile
riverboat turned between
two islands
water became rough
more like large river in flood
than ocean
captain yelled for everyone to hold on

turned riverboat into
really fast current
over cascades of white water
then riverboat beyond
edge of cascades
as if over edge of a waterfall
beyond into the sky
I was thinking this is no ordinary river
this is no ordinary riverboat
no ordinary captain
riverboat celestial craft
journey on celestial river
celestial riverboat went through the sky
like a giant bird
with no need for wings
view from pilot's chair
into the cosmos
beyond into the void
I was enjoying floating in the cosmic sea on
the cosmic riverboat
thought to myself that I had
best seat on the riverboat
even better than captain's
she chuckled listening to my thoughts
I acknowledged while I had excellent view
had no control of vessel
captain chuckled again at my thoughts
clearly non-ordinary reality cruise
on non-ordinary riverboat
with spirit realm captain
captain a goddess
unsure of her identity
celestial riverboat cruise
between two realms

two realities
to crack between the worlds
where I could look into the mysteries
into beyond
afloat on the cosmic riverboat
floating in the cosmic sea
other passengers seemed satisfied
with the ride
did not want to dangle over the edge
peer into the void
as I did
wonderful experience
wonderful memories
golden memories
golden dream
thankful for remembering
this golden dream
blessed with golden dreams

Golden Dream Fifty-four
March 16, 2013
transcribed August 27, 2013

Space Ship

little boy about six
discover bright silver 50's type
space ship
rocket ship
three or four fins below
bullet nose
lots of windows lit yellow
know the space ship
occupied with people
they are not worried
about small child playing
with their space ship like a toy
did send me calming energy
telling me to "play nice"
my first impulse had been
take toy space ship apart
look inside
inhabitants polite but clear
not to take apart their craft
do not remember anyone giving
me such a realistic toy
space ship just appeared
found in my back yard
could not see people inside
aware of their presence
as I played nice with space ship
imagined stories about where
space ship had been
images vivid spectacular
travel log of alien worlds in 3D
one after another

to fringes of space and beyond
towards end of dream
space ship people told me
they had to leave
said they had enjoyed their visit
grateful I had been careful
with their craft
which by then I knew not a toy
asked to place space ship on ground
when I did craft instantly winked out
no noise
no backlash of energy
transported to another dimension

space ship
found in my back yard
more likely it found me
images of space travel
beyond imagination
teachers
guides
wonderful dream memory

Dream Fifty-five
March 17, 2013
transcribed August 28, 2013

Old House

restoring huge old house
mansion with large grounds
carriage house gardens
hired retired building inspector
project manager
attic to be restored
to usable space first
big enough for multiple apartments
basement huge
clearing out partitions
discover additional space
basement seemed much larger
than footprint of house
wondered how far basement extended
if beyond property lines
perhaps even likely
how many subbasements
decided to make several
walk out entrances
add an elevator
whole house generator
project manager gave
excellent advice
laughed when I told him
no plasterboard no drywall
durock sheets only
heavy insulation
sound proofing
sprinkle entire house
decided to add large great room
common room

commercial kitchen
barter cooking for rent
library pool room
project manager decided
he wanted to move in when finished
told him he was first resident
I planned to live there as well
did not seem a bit worried
about cost of restoration
grounds were huge as well
equally in need of restoration
as was oversized carriage house
project manager wanted
one of suites in carriage house
told him was his
planned to replicate restoration
other mansions
high quality family style living
he would have work
as long as he wanted
he was very pleased
I was pleased to be doing
quality restorations
providing comfortable living
creating micro communities

wondering about basements
reminded me of other dreams

Dream Fifty-six
March 19, 2013
transcribed August 29, 2013

DEATH

Carol Susan leaving
my worst nightmare
come true
heartbroken devastated
I can only think about
DEATH
cruel dying
compensating for my
awake attitude
use of term disembodiment
sounds like peaceful floating
out of body
going off to otherwhere
shadow side of disembodiment
DEATH
ugly skull face grinning
blue black hag aspect of Kali
fangs dripping blood
necklace of skulls
snacking on human hearts
fresh dripping blood
compensatory dream
DEATH
reality of dying
dying to the body
death of the body
face of DEATH
not a polite nice
polysyllabic word like
disembodiment
DYING

DEATH
DEAD
Carol Susan leaving
my worst nightmare
come true

dark side of golden dreams
loss of my beloved
gone from physical realm
DYING
DEATH
DEAD
Carol Susan leaving
my worst nightmare
come true
awful dream

awful waking up discovering
dream came true
my worst nightmare
come true
Carol Susan leaving

Black Dream Fifty-seven
March 25, 2013
transcribed August 29, 2013

Carol Susan Returns

Carol Susan's radiant presence
fills our house
hear her singing
happy Spanish song
from her childhood
in another part of our house
I am so happy my beloved
has returned
say to myself
Carol Susan is back
everything is good again
life returns
love returns
my heart is back

aware that I no longer see
Carol Susan's physical body
in the dream
hear her voice singing
happy song
feel her presence
her beautiful radiant
loving presence
Carol Susan returns
not all of Carol Susan returns
her spirit returns
her body
lost and gone
forever
Carol Susan returns
different form

her spirit presence
will have to be
enough

even though not all of
Carol Susan
returns
golden dream
after black dream of yesterday
blessed with golden dreams
blessed with spirit presence
of my beloved

Golden Dream Fifty-eight
March 26, 2013
August 29, 2013

Advice

adolescent lad
middle aged woman
auburn hair
stylishly dressed
giving me fashion advice
told me to take more
interest in my appearance
particularly my clothes
not be so casual
about my attire
my appearance
she was friendly
blunt direct tough love
invested in me making
better presentation
I am interested
but not overly
polishing my external image
seems superficial
likely message
hidden in her advice

as without
so within
hell if I know
not sure I care
perhaps I should
perhaps the lesson

Dream Fifty-nine
March 29, 2013
transcribed August 29, 2013

Advising Young Souls

advisor of young souls
assisting them learn about energy
share energy as a group
energy bath
other advisors assisted
created energy field
swirled around
colors forms
expanding
illuminating
cleansing all present
advisors modulated energy
all light beings
different energies
like different sounds
swirling together
enhancing all
lovely work
advising young souls

later wondered
if they were
part of one whole

Golden Dream Sixty
March 30, 2013
transcribed August 29, 2013

Healing Bulbous Beings

Carol Susan and I along with
one of our master teachers
visiting alien world
room with
three bulbous beings
transparent bodies
semi-transparent insides
could open their bodies
like hinged silicone egg
could look directly
at mixture
in lower half of
bulbous bodies
evaluate their energy
heal any darkness
blemishes
two of bulbous beings
brighter larger
healthier than third
needed no healing
master energy healers
themselves
third smaller darker
bulbous being
needed healing
Carol Susan and I
healed smaller being
two master healers
checked our healing work
pronounced it complete
master teacher

very pleased
we thanked bulbous beings
master teacher
for
learning experience
healing expedition
alien world
alien life forms

master teacher
likely person
Carol Susan
wanted me to meet
some dreams ago
wonderful experience
being with
Carol Susan
and our
master teacher
master energy healer
working together
spirit realm healers
blessed with golden dreams

Golden Dream Sixty-one
March 31, 2013
transcribed August 30, 2013

Spirit Realm Conversation

talking to young woman
appearance of counseling session
except conversation focused on
spirit realm
young woman delighted
to find someone
to talk to about
spirit realm

brief dream
positive energy

conversation about
spirit realm
very helpful
valued conversation
for young woman

Dream Sixty-two
April 1, 2013
transcribed August 30, 2013

Group Conversation

talking to group about spirit realm
want me to tell
about my experiences
tell them not an expert
only my experiences of
spirit realm
does not make me an expert
they say that is enough
tell them their experiences
their own journeys to spirit realm
what is really important
not my stories
my stories might help recognize landscape
perhaps a bit better
nothing more
my stories shared
vicariously with others
still require their own work
their own direct experience
of spirit realm
their own stories to treasure
still want to hear my stories
vicarious experience
perhaps better than none
but not by much

Dream Sixty-three
April 1, 2013
transcribed August 30, 2013

Assessing Progress

Carol Susan and I
setting in her sanctuary
in spirit realm
she a combination of her
higher self integrated with
her recently disembodied spirit
I a combination of my
higher self not fully integrated
dream body astral body
tethered to my physical body
talking about our progress
mostly my progress
Carol Susan already removed
impurities from being embodied
traumas illnesses
loss of physical body
separation from physical realm
family friends colleagues
illumination
compassion
golden energy
golden love
I mostly focused on disembodiment
of Carol Susan
sharing our healing work
helps us both
Carol Susan further along than me
as usual
not negative or critical
our healing work connected
as we are connected

soulmatespiritmates
sharing our progress
since Carol Susan
making progress faster than me
focus more on me
Carol Susan helping me catch up
as usual
sad to always be slower one
wonderful Carol Susan
always there
encouraging
nurturing
helping me catch up
maybe I will
one day

blessed with golden dreams
visits shared with my beloved

Golden Dream Sixty-four
April 1, 2013
transcribed August 30, 2013

Blended Energy

Carol Susan and I
working together
energy healers
appear as golden rainbow dragons
matched energy healing pair
very strong healing energy
souls come into our space
garden we created
first lightly scanned
unless major darkness
given energy cleansing bath souls
always comment
on power wonderful feeling
combined energy
male female energies
full spectrum of energy balanced
combined into one
no effort
master teachers impressed
by blended skill
only master healers
can regulate energy
well enough to blend two without
turbulence
usually have to compensate
one bit stronger
one bit weaker
Carol Susan and I
blend naturally
no effort

smooth   even

side effect of our
blended healing energy
many souls
taste balanced natural
blending
effortless unity of
soulmatespiritmates
energy healers
another bonus
healing work done
in our garden
created by our
combined intent
creates special experience
special moment
not the same afterward

wonderful golden dream
shared with my beloved
blessed with golden dreams

Golden Dream Sixty-five
April 6, 2013
transcribed August 30, 2013

Grandmother Spider

Carol Susan and I at old farmstead
old house out buildings
go into one of out buildings
storage on wire mesh
in rafters
one spider
bigger than usual
black widow spider
seems unusually large
more intelligent
first impulse
let spider be
then reconsidered as
children play in
out buildings
one may get bitten
told Carol Susan I would
get spray
take care of beast
retrieve spray
return spider grown
foot across
inflated size
ability to grow much bigger
when I return with spray
spider knows my intent
spider expanding as moves
extremely quick
towards me across grid
before I can react
spider across grid

over side
leaps onto my stomach
intent on merging
I somehow intuit
grab few legs
tell spider
"oh no you don't go in there"
spider incredibly fast
merged with me before
I could react
paid no attention
to my injunction
not to merge
merged almost instantly
when I touched spider
understood my missing energy
part of me returning
part larger than physical realm life
Grandmother Spider energy
like in mythic tales
come to take up residence
in my lower abdomen
level of second chakra
understand She is
Grandmother Spider energy
ancient energy
primal force
thank Her for Her presence
Her energy
hear Grandmother Spider's
advice reactions
pleased one of Her children
accepts Her energy
acknowledges Her

thankful for Her gifts
for Her teaching
Grandmother Spider
helps travel
between worlds
Her web spans
connects
all realms

golden dream
visit to spirit realm
my beloved
Grandmother Spider
blessed with golden dreams
wonderful teachers
wonderful helpers
my beloved

Golden Dream Sixty-six
April 10, 2013
transcribed August 31, 2013

Three Dark Forces

Carol Susan and I
in garden shed
three men appear
negative intent
tell them I do not
want to hurt them
they think I am humorous
three against one
pick up bamboo rake
whack one in neck
off balance falls stunned
whack second on knee falls
tell third to help others leave
or I will stop playing nice

think three men represent
three elements
disease death loss
much more effective in dream world
than physical realm

golden dream
visit with my beloved
in spirit realm
blessed with golden dreams

Golden Dream Sixty-seven
April 20, 2013
transcribed September 1, 2013

Make Space

Carol Susan talking to me
golden radiant angel goddess
tells me I need to make space
for spirit realm Carol Susan
to take over from physical realm
Carol Susan
physical realm Carol Susan
needs to make way
for spirit realm Carol Susan

I understand message
look forward more
backward less
less focus on old memories
more on making new memories
powerful healing message
delivered by only one
I would listen to
look more with eyes of love
less with eyes of loss
can become lost in reminisces
hellfires of grief
or focus on golden dreams
making new memories
healing golden dreams
spirit realm visits
with my beloved
blessed with golden dreams

Golden Dream Sixty-eight
April 26, 2013
September 1, 2013

Together

Carol Susan busy chores errands
related to her work
I wait in conference setting
about an hour late
worried
Carol Susan arrives exhausted
physical realm appearance
we find quiet place
to sit talk
so happy to be together
talking sharing
together
so all is good

golden dream visit
with my beloved
blessed with golden dreams

Golden Dream Sixty-nine
April 29, 2013
transcribed September 1, 2013

Writing Poems

sitting at table writing poems
not clear about furnishings
room rather fuzzy
only me desk chair clear
busy writing poems
feel surrounded by people
look up all I can see are spirits
Carol Susan clearest nearest
ancestors others
all happy I am writing poems
about spirit realm
encourage me to continue
tell me time information shared
with physical realm beings
happy pleased with my work
Carol Susan Carlos Eldon
many others
presence of spirits fills room
expands into other dimensions
many spirits all agree

wonderful golden dream
blessed with golden dreams

Golden Dream Seventy
May 8, 2013
Carol Susan's Birthday
transcribed September 1, 2013

Physical Holding

Carol Susan and I
holding one another
skin to skin
kaleidoscope of holding
across many years
many lifetimes
skin against skin
no words needed
physical holding
skin to skin

woke feeling very loved
return of physical golden cocoon
golden dream
blessed with golden dreams
new memories
new experiences
woke feeling very loved

Golden Dream Seventy-one
May 14, 2013
transcribed September 1, 2013

Movie

watching movie
young Carol Susan on one side
head on my shoulder
my arm around her
young Carlos Eldon on other side
stretched out on bench seat
head near me
large black cat on my lap
I am my current age
holding Carol Susan
petting black cat
then Carlos Eldon's head
movie about loving times
Carol Susan Carlos Eldon
shared embodied together
peaceful loving experience
shared with my three
celestial angels helpers healers

watched dream with equal part
eyes of love eyes of loss coexisting
first time experienced them together
evenly matched
still point in middle
too small to enter newly formed
wonderful healing dream
healing experience
blessed with golden dreams

Golden Dream Seventy-two
May 22, 2013
transcribed September 2, 2013

Healing Work

Carol Susan and I sitting in
our private sanctuary
Carol Susan telling me about her work
tells me about very upset woman
confused surprised disappointed
heaven not as described in Bible
Carol Susan helping her adjust
her expectations
question what she had been taught
believed in so intensely
for so many years
woman resistant to accept
her new circumstances
in limbo of her belief system
heaven she found wonderful place
but felt betrayed by her teachings
deceived by her beliefs
Carol Susan helping her heal
her compassionate loving presence
helping woman's heart open
let go of old heaven
embrace new heaven
Carol Susan very happy doing
celestial healing work
I was very happy to be visiting
with my beloved
hearing about her celestial work
sharing her celestial experiences
wonderful golden dream
blessed with golden dreams

Golden Dream Seventy-three
May 30, 2013
transcribed September 2, 2013

Multiple Witnesses

witnessing Carol Susan's disembodiment
with three sets of eyes

Carol Susan's celestial self
Carlos Eldon's celestial self
watching Carol Susan's disembodiment

physically present
holding Carol Susan
just before her disembodiment
physical Carlos Eldon
holding watching
my beloved Carol Susan
final stages of disembodiment

my embodied soul witnessing
Carol Susan's disembodiment
active participant
aware of others

multiple witnesses
multiple levels of experience
intensely painful to witness
Carol Susan's disembodiment
from any perspective

as Carol Susan laid back
took her last breath
two celestial beings
infinite compassion for all
departing spirit of Carol Susan

two left behind
compassionate love of angels
golden rainbow dragons
goddess and god
for their children
sending healing love
healing energy
compassionate love
beyond description
beyond words

my embodied soul
witnessed heart of my hearts
breaking in two
larger portion of my heart
heart of my hearts
remained connected to
Carol Susan's departing spirit
as her now disembodied soul
traveled through portal
to spirit realm
leaving behind much diminished
Carlos Eldon

three kinds of seeing
three sets of eyes
separate yet one
all experiencing intense trauma
of Carol Susan's disembodiment
physical eyes
embodied soul eyes
celestial eyes
all sharing the worst experience
Carol Susan's disembodiment

all our ancestors others witnessing
sharing the experience

very intense dream experience
very painful dream experience
healing energy as well
celestial compassionate love
golden dream
blessed with golden dreams

Golden Dream Seventy-four
May 31, 2013
transcribed September 2, 2013

White Tara

presence of White Tara
Carol Susan Maya Merlin
Taryne Jade intermittently
me merged with my celestial self
Carol Susan young radiant beautiful
celestial angel goddess
White Tara showering
everyone with Her
compassionate love
Carol Susan seems to host
Taryne Jade intermittently
White Tara pleased with everyone
almost like a celestial grandmother
relaxed peaceful setting
paradise
radiant golden energy

wonderful golden dream
blessed with golden dreams

Golden Dream Seventy-five
June 2, 2013
transcribed September 2, 2013

Celestial Bounty Hunters

Carol Susan Taryne Jade and me
riding in country
guide points out small road
way to secrete installation
turn into narrow road
seems little used
travel through small forest
trees over road
going through tunnel
coming out of forest
large expanse rolling hills meadows
road between two hills
emerges in abandon mining area
buildings dilapidated
guide says part of disguise
directs us to specific building
enter inside clean well maintained
gold smelting facility
Carol Susan Taryne Jade and I
celestial detectives
celestial bounty hunters
charged with finding fugitives
while Carol Susan and Taryne Jade
look at a series of doors
little Maya shows up
happy she has tracked us
to secret facility
doors lead to alternative realms
Carol Susan and Taryne Jade
know correct door
enter a new landscape

small house
fugitive appears with what looks like
a handheld Gatling gun
but is a plasma weapon
shoots energy balls
that stun or disable
fugitive fires plasma weapon
repeatedly rapid fire at
Carol Susan and Taryne Jade
they deflect plasma balls
Carol Susan sends two back
to fugitive
strikes him in stomach
surprised as he fell
disabled on the ground
Carol Susan and Taryne Jade
appear unarmed
my job to watch fugitive while
Carol Susan and Taryne Jade
do something else
fugitive suddenly slithers
against old wooden building
collapses on him
he is under wooden frame
not too badly hurt
leave him there to wait
he yells for help
woman comes from small house
batwoman with wands
throwing boas charged with energy
younger man with her
known Taryne Jade years before
Carol Susan and Taryne Jade return
fugitive's helpers uncertain what to do

Carol Susan and Taryne Jade tells them
we are there to apprehend fugitive
send him back to his tribunal
he could travel across realms dimensions
did some unkindly things in another realm
unacceptable to his tribunal
now he must return
explain his conduct
Carol Susan Taryne Jade and I
collectors of errant souls
who misuse their gifts of traveling
across time and realms
fugitive's helpers decide
they would not interfere
with fugitive's tribunal
very wise decision
we extract man
from under the rubble
Carol Susan concentrated his energy
puts him into cylinder
opens portal
sent him to his tribunal
we retrace our travel
emerge at entrance
to mine building
Maya waiting
happy to see us

curious dream
golden dream
blessed with golden dreams

Golden Dream Seventy-six
June 7, 2013
transcribed September 2, 2013

No Awards

invited to banquet
turns out to be awards ceremony
for Carol Susan's helpers healers
offensive to me since none succeeded
my name called I refuse to accept
tell group ceremony offensive to me
since everyone failed including me
in the end Carol Susan saved herself
from her failing physical body
by disembodiment only choice she had
several large chaps
come to bring me to dais
I poked them in throats
not to hurt them
only disable temporarily
tell group next person
tries to force me
will have trouble getting up

sad angry dream world
suggested award for
failed healers
unacceptable concept
no award for me

Dark Dream Seventy-seven
June 14, 2013
transcribed September 2, 2013

Spirit Warrior

Carol Susan and I setting together
she telling me about her physical limitations
result of her illness
Carol Susan speaking with
equanimity
not frustration anger or bitterness
acceptance
true spirit warrior
accepted her fate
hard won struggle
powerful spirit warrior
Carol Susan mostly distressed
about leaving her family
her physical embodiment
abbreviated
even in dreaming
I am in denial about
pending disembodiment

remembering the dream
writing it down
told Carol Susan
"I send you all my love
do not know anything else I can do"
Carol Susan says "it is enough"
thank you

Golden Dream Seventy-eight
June 25, 2013
transcribed September 2, 2013

Meaningful Work

Carol Susan and I sitting together
at our kitchen table
working on quarterly financials
DeVaney-Wong International
activity we shared many years
I was always happy
Carol Susan created meaningful work
master facilitator
therapist healer
I was always proud
of her accomplishments
more proud her work
had heart soul
meaningful work
in the dream we are
very comfortable sharing the task
intense love of companions
soulmates

writing down the dream
remembering intense yet comfortable
companionship of embodied soulmates
now even more aware
our embodied togetherness
treasure beyond measure
love of embodied soulmates
wonderful golden dream
blessed with golden dreams

Golden Dream Seventy-nine
June 29, 2013
transcribed September 2, 2013

Nightmare

dream reliving horror of
Carol Susan's illness
treatments
disembodiment
vague symptoms
multiple hospitalizations
emergency stent
major surgery
recovery
chemo
reoccurrence
more chemo
metastasize
more surgery
infection
weaker
more pain
all the while
Carol Susan rarely complained
offered others support
encouragement
loving energy
her wonderful compassion
living moment to moment
then her beautiful radiant spirit
left her physical body
no longer capable of containing
her spirit any longer

dream at twenty months
since disembodiment

twenty long months
not a golden dream
nightmare
thought I relived awake
often enough
guess not
no one calls them daymares
reality of my experience
waking nightmares
black dream
twenty months
nightmare

Black Dream Eighty
July 1, 2013
transcribed September 2, 2013

Fourth Grade Teacher

celestial version of fourth grade
taught by a goddess
fourth grade teacher
not what she seemed
words not necessary
relaxed loving atmosphere
support encouragement wisdom
very special helper
taught by a goddess
goddess of compassion
multiple faces
fourth grade teacher
Carol Susan
others
pantheon of goddesses
of compassion

golden dream
blessed with golden dreams

Golden Dream Eighty-one
July 4, 2013
transcribed September 3, 2013

Recharging

Carol Susan Taryne Jade and I
upscale restaurant nice table
restaurant very crowded
we are responsible for protecting
small spaceship celestial craft
seems experiencing problems
with energy systems
small spaceship hovering
find small unused room for spaceship
tell people Taryne Jade's science project
celebrating won an award
concerned about spaceship
someone might disrupt recharging
spend much of evening
watching over craft
towards closing time
occupants of craft announce
energy systems repaired
ready to depart wish them well
thank them for their visit
then they are gone
ask Carol Susan if she would
like to go some where
get something to eat
since spent evening
watching over craft
did not order food
place so busy no one noticed
Carol Susan laughs agrees

atmosphere of restaurant

positive relaxed
seems if all people family
ancestors even staff
family gathering
on one curious about science project
craft that hovered no sound
unknown energy source

craft only appeared to be
recharging and repairing energy system
actually recharging repairing
energy systems of
Carol Susan Taryne Jade and me
all others in restaurant
occupants in craft energy healers
very complex healing system
yet amazingly simple
craft sent out loving healing energy
balancing bodies' energy centers
cellular level healing
chakra cleaning balancing recharging
incomprehensible to mind
body experienced healing energy
soul experienced restoration
of harmony balance
between energy centers
recharging

wonderful golden dream
blessed with golden dreams

Golden Dream Eighty-two
July 4, 2013
transcribed September 3, 2013

Ancestors Checking

Carol Susan one of our ancestors and me
together going to restaurant
ancestor says only be here a moment
checking on me
make sure I am in good hands
Carol Susan with me
ancestor says I have very best
ancestors do not need to worry
then says not hungry
so he will leave
we all laugh at his humor
eating astral realm food
Carol Susan stayed
we did not need to eat either
our food energy of love
nurturance companionship
I am always so happy
to visit with Carol Susan
in dream time
be together
Carol Susan beside me
enough
much more than enough
possession in great measure

wonderful golden dream
blessed with golden dreams

Golden Dream Eighty-three
July 5, 2013
transcribed September 3, 2013

Work Questions

questioned at work
esoteric governmental regulations
used to know
expert
now can recall very little
unconcerned by my inability
questioners surprised by my
lack of knowledge
even more surprised by my
lack of concern
lack of interest
make no effort to answer questions
no interest in questions
not interested in that kind of work
not a path with heart
not my soul's path
not my soul's way

refreshing dream
kind of work behind me
other priorities
matters of soul spirit

golden dream
blessed with golden dreams

Golden Dream Eighty-four
July 11, 2013
transcribed September 3, 2013

Alone

Carol Susan somewhere else
with group of people
otherwhere spirit realm
ancestors others
I am alone
spirit realm sanctuary
missing my sweetheart
she disembodied I am embodied
miss her being embodied
too much for words
too much for tears
miss her too much
alone
miss her physical body
know she is with me
spirit presence
still miss her too much
looking from eyes of loss
feel alone part true
looking from eyes of love
not alone
alone not alone
paradoxically both true
depends how I look
eyes I use
heart of my hearts knows
embodies soul knows
I am not alone

Dream Eighty-five
July 12, 2013
transcribed September 3, 2013

Cottage Project

dream takes place during
visit to our cottage
in dream designing
patio or deck
in rear of cottage
patio of stone
or raised deck
voice tells me raised deck
above water mud
eventually screen in
dream suggests using
hard rough rubber boards
for floor

do not know why
dream seems important
perhaps housekeeping dream
following my waking ruminations
projects for our cottage
talked about with Carol Susan
perhaps something more
place to set in
cottage's expanding garden
place of positive energy
do not know

Dream Eighty-six
July 26, 2013
transcribed September 3, 2013

Conference

observer at conference
watching from behind
conference commentator
young Asian woman
working hard to make
conference seem interesting relevant
small conference casual atmosphere
attendees mostly old white men
old boys club telling stories
boring even themselves
half hearted attempts
reinforce each other's importance
stripped down essence
of many conferences
no matter how dressed up
attendees rather be on vacation
many are missing
one presenter told how much
he and his family enjoyed
drive on Skyland Drive
on the way to conference
high point of conference for him

only redeeming feature of dream
young Asian woman
positive life force
positive energy

Dream Eighty-seven
July 31, 2013
transcribed September 3, 2013

Tar Pit Balance

colleague walks into pond
tar pit type pond
gets stuck drowns
try to rescue him
no success

two furry "little people"
walk into tar pit pond
get stuck drown
try to rescue them
no success

colleague personification of
rationality
two furry little people
personifications of
primitive animal instincts
sacrifice two extremes
find balance in middle
not overly intellectual
not overly instinctual
balance

water over earth
hidden danger
ground not always
what it seems
proceed with caution

Dream Eighty-eight
August 6, 2013
transcribed September 3, 2013

Not A Tourist

dream starts in old city physical realm
changes to celestial realm city
vibrant white gold rainbow colors
inhabitants dressed in white gold
splash of color
all young radiant with energy
I am young wearing bright white shirt
shinning black pants shoes
upper half matches residents
not lower half
yet not totally of physical realm
can see what appears to be
tourists on edge of city
looking in
dressed in browns greens
only on edge looking in
I am in middle of city
wondering around
see carriage two young men
leading strange creature
creature towing carriage
creature mostly energy
rainbow colored with golden aura
cat-like with dragon features
intends carriage to follow
not really towing
unless by intent
in distance giant Farris wheel
mood festive celebration
I am half of this realm
half of another

dream seems blend of two
one superimposed over other
scenes flickering with
spirit realm predominate
not a tourist
not resident either
lower spirit realm than
my usual visits
younger souls
playing with energy
learning through play
unsure they can see me
had feeling I would be
some of these young souls
teacher guide elder
in my celestial form
Carol Susan as well
teachers guides healers
elders
at point of dream
young souls enjoying
playing with energy
learning about spirit realm

golden dream
blessed with golden dreams

Golden Dream Eighty-nine
August 11, 2013
transcribed September 4, 2013

Speeding Tickets

Carol Susan and I driving back
from funeral
going bit fast did not hear
Carol Susan advise me to slow down
got ticket speeding 30 in 25
told officer just trying to go home
after yet another funeral
officer said "didn't I just give you
a ticket for same thing less than
a month ago"
"yes another funeral just trying
to get home"
officer said "I am sorry to have to
give you another ticket but you
know rules are rules"
I suggested he could give me
warning considering
circumstances
he gave me a ticket
back in car
Carol Susan said
"I told you we should have called
1-800-DRIVE4U
since you were preoccupied"
at first was going to complain
about not hearing any advice
then I realized she had given
me that advice on both occasions
my hearing loss combined with
my hardheadedness
got me into trouble again

realized Carol Susan had
almost always given me
excellent advice
over many years
which I did not always follow
sometimes did not even hear
sometimes too hardheaded
to listen
at end of dream
I am telling Carol Susan
I am sorry I did not listen
or follow her advice
promise to do better
going forward

I Ching recommended
being receptive
open mouth to receive
nourishment physical spiritual
realize speeding tickets
for going faster than appropriate
miss seeing hearing
messages
too fast to perceive
subtle spirit realm
messages
slowing down another way
being more receptive

Golden Dream Ninety
August 17, 2013
transcribed September 4, 2013

Wiser

getting ready to do chores
run errands
Carol Susan not feeling well
stay home with her
hold her comfort her
give her loving energy
she felt better
I did too
remember thinking I was
growing wiser
listening to my heart
not my head
decisions from my heart
soul's priorities
heart of my heart priorities
growing wiser
in dream we are young
in physical realm

occurred early in physical realm
open heart pathway to wisdom
Carol Susan was excellent teacher
taught by example
open heart
soul's priorities
wise at early age
grateful for my teacher's
heart centered ways

Golden Dream Ninety-one
August 18, 2013
transcribed September 4, 2013

Carol Susan's Necklace

making Carol Susan a necklace
large round diamonds
large round rubies
each size of large marble
could have made them bigger
ping pong ball size
ostentatious
as jewels smooth round
added light to each one
so each glowed from inside
placed golden aura around strand
Carol Susan came in
as I was manifesting jewels
knew what it was going to be
asked how I planned
to get them to stay together
as a strand
since jewels had no holes
"with intent" I answered
"my love will hold them together"

diamond "pearls"
ruby "pearls"
alternating
diamonds for strength purity
rainbow of colors
ruby for fire passion
energy spirit blood
necklace creation of my love
Carol Susan very pleased
with my gift

told her after she wore it a while
would be absorbed by her energy
become part of her energy
absorbed as pure love
Carol Susan very happy
with my love
I was very happy
to give it to her

Golden Dream Ninety-two
August 18, 2013
transcribed September 4, 2013

Double Booked

arrived at acupuncturist
another chap there
for his appointment
younger chap
seem acupuncturist
double booked
also running late
we sit talk
tell him I am retired
open schedule
so will be happy
to defer appointment to him
reschedule
he does not want to
take my appointment
reminds me of myself years ago
tells me about a supplement
does wonders for him
thinks I should give it a try
acupuncturist arrives
feeling ill perhaps contagious
wants to reschedule both of us
we laugh at resolution
leave on our separate ways
dream meeting younger
version of myself mid-twenties
very comfortable energy
between us

Dream Ninety-three
August 18, 2013
transcribed September 4, 2013

Old One

one of the old ones
ancestor grandfather
sitting in celestial garden
talking with young souls
comfortable atmosphere
young souls comfortable
with old one
asking questions sharing stories
sharing energy
I tell few stories
encourage others to share
nurture young souls
encourage them to nurture
themselves each other
I accept each fully
exactly where they are
in their development
metamorphosis
energy field created
encourages growth
development
lovely to experience
being old one
master healer
master facilitator
old alchemist grown up
lovely golden dream
blessed with golden dreams

Golden Dream Ninety-four
August 30, 2013
transcribed September 4, 2013

Waiting In Line

older waiting in line
governmental offices
long line forms as names called
some people cut in front of others
workers witness shake their heads
young woman steps in front of me
I remark unfortunate manners
so out of fashion
she surprised I spoke to her
tell her since she is in a hurry
no problem if she goes ahead of me
I am retired in no hurry
my energy very calm accepting
my offer sincere
people in line seem to be less frantic
take a collective deep breath
order name called not place in line
protocol anyway
no gain cutting in line
frantic pace of everyday life
prevents cultivation of
more meaningful life
more soulful life
more heart centered life
unfortunate waiting in line
could be different experience

Dream Ninety-five
August 30, 2013
transcribed September 5, 2013

151

Green Spiral Member

young lad early adolescent
playing with bright green wrapping ribbon
whirled into spiral
about three feet long
stick in top front of pants
dangles down like
green spiral member
dance prance about
friend with me laughing
I am laughing too
as I zoom about

at first dream seems silly
antics of fool rather than Fool
Trickster aspect wakens
more energy play
message seems to be lighten up
enjoy playing
whirling dancing prancing
alien concepts to my mood
waking attitude
compensatory
at first thought just antics of
silly immature adolescent
perhaps so
perhaps deeper meaning
recapturing energy
play fun joy
enthusiasm of adolescent
been mostly missing
long time gone

all but forgotten
lost and gone forever
still available in dreams
obviously not totally gone

Dream Ninety-six
August 31, 2013
transcribed September 5, 2013

Energy Assessment

conducting energy assessment
reading energy of each chakra
physical body first
each subtle energy body in turn
energy better at more subtle bodies
further away from physical body
physical body most energy problems
energy blocks poor flow constricted
not surprising finding considering
traumas large small
dark times energy more blocked
no outlets no releases
energy flows all but frozen
anticipatory grief
then black times
hellfires of grief
no energy except to grieve
nothing else much matters
life seems empty meaningless
then golden dreams
slowly healing energy blocks
healing energy constrictions
slow painful process
blessed with healing golden dreams
dream visits to spirit realm
my beloved

Dream Ninety-seven
September 2, 2013
transcribed September 5, 2013

Productivity Assessment

in the dream conducting
productivity assessment
not chores or tasks of daily living
soulful productivity
healing work
soul's work
care and feeding of my soul
Carol Susan's Taryne Jade's
others
hellfires of grief grieving
establishing shrine
observances
lighting candles
lighting incense
other ceremonies
journaling
dream journaling
wrote *Hellfires I*
writing **Golden Dreams**
writing *Hellfires II*
being receptive to spirit realm
heart of my heart
serving my experiences
so my experiences will serve me
grieving
golden dream visits to spirit realm
my beloved

Dream Ninety-eight
September 2, 2013
transcribed September 5, 2013

Note: My thanks to Alberto Villoldo for the concept of serving your
experience so your experience will serve you

Reassurance

had been working on *Golden Dreams*
written first eighty dreams
transcribed into poems
seventeen left in dream journal
only 97 dreams
need 14 more to have 111
by October 31, 2013
second year anniversary
Carol Susan's disembodiment
started to worry
tired
decided to take a nap

awoke from nap remembering
dream
ancestors telling me
reassuring me
do not have to worry
will be enough dreams
will work out
Golden Dreams will be completed
ready to be placed on the shrine
by October 31, 2013
wonderful reassurance
wonderful golden dream
grateful for ancestors
reassurance
blessed with golden dreams

Golden Dream Ninety-nine
September 2, 2013
transcribed September 5, 2013

Portal

outside luminous radiant city
city inside clear energy bubble
invisible bubble
yet my metasenses aware
city in spirit realm
celestial city
bubble represents veil
dream makes clear
portal to spirit realm   dreams
dreaming self crosses veil
energy bubble
as if nonexistent
dreaming self showing me
answer to my search
how to part the veil   awake
automatic for dreaming self
veil does not exist
know dreaming self visits
spirit realm often
even when I am awake
just do not remember
awake
forgetting mechanism stronger
imposes flatland perspective on
spirit realm experience
spirit realm memories
reduces them into nonexistence

guided tour by my dreaming self
so my waking self can fully
experience know understand

dreaming major portal to spirit realm
dreaming self experiences no veil
dreaming self not limited to dreamtime
journey to spirit realm
not limited to dreams
travels back and forth at will
my waking self forgets these
journeys adventures memories
perhaps shadows of memories
linger in
daydreams fantasies musings
intuitions whispers messages
my quest redefined refined
quest not to cross the veil awake
dreaming self already does at will
quest to remember
strengthen remembering mechanism
weaken forgetting mechanism
I Ching advises being receptive
open to nourishment
from physical spirit realms
dreaming self
celestial self agree

golden dream one hundred
very powerful message
wonderful assistance
redefines my quest
grateful for golden dreams
blessed with golden dreams

Golden Dream One Hundred
September 5, 2013

Black Panther

Carol Susan large black panther
laying on sofa
modern black leather
room similar to her sanctuary
relaxing
purring
talking with me
mind to mind
sharing our energy
sharing our love
spirit black panther
golden aura
radiant rainbow colors
wonderful visiting my beloved
another of her forms
celestial black panther
golden dream
blessed with golden dreams

Golden Dream One hundred-one
September 6, 2013

Old Friends

enter bathroom area upscale hotel
young woman her parents
sleeping in lounge area
go to facilities section
young man asleep one of the stalls
baby with him sleeping too
she opens her eyes when I arrive
senses me somehow
grows into a toddler
little girl right before my eyes
smiles walks over to me
she knows me
I know her
old friends
young mother arrives
embarrassed daughter bothering me
tell her we have know each other
very long time
old friends
many life times
young mother smiles
does not seem to notice
young girl aged two or three years
during her nap
I was not surprised either
aura between us generated
accelerated growth
time shift
wrinkle in fabric of time
dream ends little girl
her mother wondering off

know we will meet again
always forever and beyond
golden dream
blessed with golden dreams

Golden Dream One Hundred two
September 6, 2013

Writing Poems II

dream begins
kaleidoscopic whirl of images
too fast to identify
slows down
one image

sitting at table writing poems
around me Carol Susan
celestial Carlos Eldon
all our ancestors
helpers healers
master helpers healers
all happy smiling
nodding their heads in approval
my continued writing
wonderful loving golden energy
wonderful experience
wonderful memory
beyond words

golden dream
grateful for golden dreams
blessed with golden dreams

Golden Dream One hundred three
September 8, 2013

Note: *Writing Poems* is Golden Dream Seventy, May 8, 2013, page 112

Umbrella

in hotel lobby
waiting for Carol Susan
in meeting across street
raining
have my umbrella
plan to meet Carol Susan
when she comes out
shelter her from rain
she appears
I wave hold up umbrella
signal her to wait
she waves smiles understands
open umbrella
no fabric only ribs
start out anyway

at my first step
scene changes
lovely garden
Carol Susan sitting
waiting for me
I walk to her
we embrace
I sit beside her
tell her about umbrella
missing fabric
open umbrella
black and white fabric
completely restored
better than new
tell Carol Susan

anything in our energy field
healed
even umbrellas
we laugh
enjoying being together

writing down dream
first part physical realm
could not protect Carol Susan
from rain
much worse things
my umbrella non functional
garden spirit realm
Carol Susan did not need
to be protected
perfect just way she is

sad I could not shelter
Carol Susan from life's adversities
in physical realm
grateful to visit with her
spirit realm garden
wonderful golden dream
blessed with golden dreams

Golden Dream One hundred four
September 12, 2013

Intersection/Portal

overlooking intersection
from balcony
others observing
demonstration of transporting
emergency vehicle
approaches intersection
using intent of driver
transport ambulance to ER
observers ask if driver disoriented
with instantaneous arrival at ER
explain driver will believe
mind playing tricks
too intent on getting to ER
observers satisfied

intersection portal between
physical spirit realms
folding space
compressing space
folding time
fast forwarding time
unsure purpose of demonstration
observers satisfied with
demonstration and explanation
spirit realm function
in physical realm

Dream One Hundred-five
September 15, 2013

168

Fifteen Year Olds

Carol Susan and I fifteen year olds
mixture of embodied souls
astral bodies
celestial energies
other aspects
visiting astral realm version
store I worked after school
beautiful golden radiant fifteen year olds
two higher selves watching
arrive on third floor
toy department when I was young
floor littered with toys
step carefully to avoid toys
navigate obstacle course
holding hands laughing
about path we take around toys
Carol Susan telling me in this life time
she will not be able to grow old with me
I did not like hearing that
tell her we will navigate that
just like obstacles on the floor
she not as certain

not in physical realm
not embodied fifteen year olds
both beautiful radiant energy beings
Carol Susan beautiful young goddess
I beautiful young god
golden energy
golden power
wonderful to see pair

celestial fifteen year olds
yin yang
alchemical couple
young Queen young King
not in alchemical crucible
in our golden cocoon
pure energy of love

have always had subtle knowing
Carol Susan's soul and mine
always present in each other's lives
subtle presences always with
one another

complicated dream
hard to reduce
images to words
multiple layers of reality
multiple realities
celestial selves watching
others helpers teachers masters
watching Carol Susan and I
crossing obstacle course
image of dance of life
dancing across floor of time
we did not touch floor
so much power energy golden love
we floated above obstacles
danced across in air
in our golden cocoon
above obstacles
so much golden energy
so much golden love
did not want dream to end

did not want to stop writing
in our dream journal
extract all golden energy
wonderful golden dream
golden nourishment of love
wonderful golden experience
dancing above floor of time
in our golden cocoon
wonderful golden memory
wonderful golden dream
blessed with golden dreams
visits to spirit realm
with my beloved

Golden Dream One hundred six
September 21, 2013

Spirit Embrace

Carol Susan and I
embrace in spirit realm
images from Carol Susan
elegant images
words simplify complexity of images
Carol Susan did not want
to leave her love ones behind
so much compassionate love
tell her I know understand
sorry she had to leave so early
we kissed
images from Carol Susan
misses some of physical experiences
being embodied in physical realm
not pain or
suffering of disease

on surface simple dream
sharing embrace kiss
sharing of images
too complex for words
compelled to offer
dream experience
dream memory
as best as I can

Carol Susan did not want
to leave her loved ones behind
though disembodied
she has not left her
loved ones behind

her spirit form surrounds
all of her loved ones
some experience her subtle energies
from spirit realm
more easily than others
some have little facility for
experiencing spirit realm
been trained since childhood
deny existence of other realities
separate realities
other forms of being
spirit realm by whatever name

wistful moment
missing physical sensations
of physical body
know she has not left
her loved ones behind
only changed to more
subtle form
wonderful golden dream
blessed with golden dreams
spirit realm visits
with my beloved

Golden Dream One hundred seven
September 22, 2013

Ancient Teachers

walking in woods
suddenly realize entered
ancient forest
follow animal trail
energy very positive
sacred forest
primordial forest
come to clearing
meadow
middle of forest
center of meadow
huge ancient tree
resting in Grandmother Tree
huge ancient dragon
earthtone golden dragon
Grandmother Dragon
I apologize for entering
Their space without
asking Their permission
tell me I am welcome
tell Grandmother Dragon
I am not much of a snack
small little energy
little meat little protein
Grandmother Dragon chuckles
tells me She does not eat
sentient beings
any physical food
energy being pure energy
as is Grandmother Tree
tell Them I am honored to be

in Their presences
Grandmother Dragon says
I have a way with words
more courageous than I realize
did not see Her as
terrible evil monster
told Her I was not worth
Her trouble to eat
She found humorous
knew I was teasing
knew I had moved beyond
medieval myth of knight
rescuing damsel in distress
slaying evil dragon
told Grandmother Dragon
I had written about that
She said She knew
watched read my writing
part of why I was welcome
my wish to befriend dragons
rescue dragons from medieval myth
create modern hero's myth
new myth all heroes
no heroes
no heroes needed
embrace dragon and maiden
Grandmother Dragon chuckles
Grandmother Tree also
both agree to be my allies teachers
I thank Them

while Carol Susan not visible
her presence always with me
mine always with her

as above so below
as within so without
Grandmother Dragon
Grandmother Tree
powerful teachers
realize I have been with
my ancient teachers
many lifetimes
just have not remembered
Grandmother Dragon
changes forms colors
Carol Susan and I her children
golden rainbow dragons
always forever and beyond
powerful dream
golden dream
grateful for golden dreams
blessed with golden dreams

.

Golden Dream One hundred eight
September 23, 2013

Mystery Woman

sitting with woman with auburn hair
know her
other dreams
do not remember her name
mystery woman
elegant mature woman
beautiful radiant
golden energy of love
talking mind to mind
do not remember conversation
master teacher
does not look like
anyone I know
exactly

perhaps
goddess of compassion
in disguise
Kuan Yin
White Tara
Mother Mary
another aspect of Carol Susan
although Carol Susan sitting
with Taryne Jade
at another table
still possible
they recognize
mystery woman with auburn hair

perhaps
one of the grandmothers
in disguise
talking mind to mind
preparation for something
do not remember conversation
unknown mysteries
mystery woman
mystery teaching
mystery preparation

my work to be
receptive
compassionate
persevere
working on patience

mystery golden dream
grateful for golden dreams
blessed with golden dreams

Golden Dream One hundred nine
September 26, 2013

Carol Susan and Old House

been traveling unknown regions
return to our old house
huge house
many rooms
many levels
go to upper level first
Carol Susan resting on our bed
young radiant beautiful goddess
glad to see me
delighted to see her
she jumps up
we embrace
she wearing
black jade dragon pendent
gave her 1977
Carol Susan takes it off
puts it on me
tells me she wants
me to wear
black jade dragon
awhile
protection
positive energy
so happy to see her
feel our embrace
accept her gift
black jade dragon pendent
gave her 1977

next wandering around old house
lower level offices

my office seems to have been
unused for quite some time
dining room much like one
met older woman with auburn hair
spoke mind to mind
preparing me for something
my conscious mind does not remember
embodied soul knows of course
not telling either
at least not in language
I understand

someone installed water fountain
in dining room
found that a bit strange
first floor level does seem
more like public space
surprised to see water fountain
formal dining room
perhaps room too dry
needed hydration
my office unused
another public space
seem to have retired
from public realm
travel to otherwhere
top of house portal to
spirit realm
my beloved Carol Susan
when I return to lower levels
seems like I am almost a stranger
in my own physical realm house
only others clear in dream
Carol Susan

energy remnants of
older woman with auburn hair
they could be the same

wonderful being with Carol Susan
in spirit realm
spirit realm embrace
her gift of protection
energy love
know I visit often
do not always
remember
only need to climb
into upper level
our old house
portal to spirit realm
my beloved

wonderful golden dream
blessed with golden dreams
grateful for golden dreams

Golden Dancing

Carol Susan and I at a
cantina dance hall in Panama
rustic setting golden energy
sitting in upper level
dance floor below
group of musicians appears
start to play Panamian folk music
hold out my hand to Carol Susan
no words needed
she takes my hand
spin her about few times
she laughs
singing along in Spanish
lovely voice
beautiful young goddess
we descend steps
whirl her about
dancing to music
Carol Susan pleased with
my enthusiastic dancing
not much of a dancer in
physical realm
excellent dancer in
spirit realm
Carol Susan laughing
throws herself into music
with her customary abandon
both enjoying music dancing
dancing beyond setting sun
beyond rising moon
beyond stars

dancing into
always forever and beyond

wonderful golden dream
blessed with golden dreams
visits to spirit realm
dancing with my beloved

Golden Dream One hundred eleven
October 9, 2013

Acknowledgements

Celestial Helpers-Healers:
Carol Susan, Carlos Eldon, and others

Embodied Helpers-Healers:
Carol Susan, Carlos Eldon, Taryne Jade, Denise Conner, Maya and Merlin, Johanna Moorman, Carol Pollock, Nancy Powell, Deb Cannon, Alice Claussen, Dede Dancing, and others

Taylor DeVaney Wong Family Support:
Especially Taryne Jade, Bob, Martha, Itzel, Manuella, Mater, Doris, Diana, Carmen, Alfonso, Fanny and Tommy, Ceci, Chicho, and others

Authors

Carlos Eldon Taylor is a psychotherapist licensed as a Licensed Professional Counselor (LPC-Virginia), Licensed Mental Health Counselor (LMHC-Florida), and National Certified Counselor. None of which was much help when it became his turn to experience the hellfires of grief and dark nights of the soul after the disembodiment of his beloved Carol Susan. Shortly after they met Carol Susan transformed Charles Eldon into Carlos Eldon saying it is a better fit.

Carol Susan DeVaney-Wong was a psychotherapist licensed as a Licensed Clinical Social Worker (LCSW-Virginia), nationally Certified Social Worker (ACSW-NASW), Certified Professional Facilitator (International Association of Facilitators), Certified Professional in Learning and Performance (CPLP-ASTD), and a United Nations Preferred Provider. Carol Susan established her consulting company DeVaney-Wong International in 1989 and maintained a successful consulting practice for over twenty years. For additional information about Carol Susan's embodied life and work visit her memorial web site at www.devaneywong.com. On October 31, 2011 Carol Susan's beautiful radiant spirit disembodied to return to the spirit realm.

It is difficult to describe a spirit realm energy being using physical realm terms as words can only convey the edges of the experience. Carol Susan is a beautiful radiant golden angel-goddess-celestial healer-golden rainbow dragon mother goddess and more...much more.

Contact Information
celdontaylor@gmail.com

www.ingramcontent.com/pod-product-compliance
Lightning Source LLC
LaVergne TN
LVHW011156080426
835508LV00007B/442